Eve
1!

News for every

**Vietnamese 'boat people' refugees
rescued by the US Navy, December 1979.**

By Hugh Morrison

MONTPELIER PUBLISHING
LONDON

Front cover (clockwise from left): Britain's Prime Minister Margaret Thatcher with US President Jimmy Carter. The Skylab space station. Paul and Linda McCartney. The 'smiling sun' Anti-nuclear energy campaign logo (courtesy of Ann Lund).

Back cover (clockwise from top): Britain's Prime Minister James Callaghan. Mother Theresa of Calcutta. Sid Vicious of 'The Sex Pistols'. Artist's impression of the Pioneer probe reaching Saturn. The Sony Walkman. The 1979 Ford Pinto.

Image credits: Mario Casciano, Anefo/Croes RC, Rob Bogaerts, Alan Light, Riksarkivet/National Archives of Norway, Hans Van Djiek/Anefo, David Hume Kennerly/Gerald Ford Archive, Jordy Schaap, MG Lindee, Montanabw, NASA, Warren K Leffler, Jimmy Baikovicius, Archives New Zealand, R McGuire, Georges Biard, Koen Syuk/Anefo, David Dixon, Jim Summaria, Jeremy Gilbert, Eric Koch/Anefo, Marcel Antonisse/Anefo, Bill Fitzpatrick, Binary Sequence, Phil Eggman, Donn Dughi, Sipuede7, Fanny Schertzer, William Gottlieb, Mario Dibiasi, Allan Warren, Alan Light, Htonl, Fototeca Online a Comunismului Românesc, Knocko, Thomas J O'Halloran, University of Houston, Elektra, Hans Weingartz, Manfredo Ferrari, Jack 1956, Marion S Trikosko, Michael Dorausch, Joost Evers, Pratyeka, Ignis, Avro, Evan Amos, Anne Lund.

ISBN: 9781090923820

Published in Great Britain by Montpelier Publishing, London.

Distributed by Amazon Createspace/KDP.

Events of
1979

News for every day of the year

Monday 1: The United Nations International Year of the Child begins. Pop group ABBA write the song *Chiquitita* to commemorate the event.

Tuesday 2: The trial of Sid Vicious of the Sex Pistols begins, for the murder of his girlfriend Nancy Spungeon.

Wednesday 3: Guillermo Vilas beats John Marks in the 67th Men's Australian Open tennis tournament.

Thursday 4: The state of Ohio agrees to pay $675,000 in compensation to those injured when the National Guard fired on demonstrators at Kent State University in 1970.

Friday 5: US jazz bassist and composer Charles Mingus dies aged 56.

Saturday 6: *YMCA* by the Village People reaches number one in the British pop charts.

Sunday 7: The People's Army of Vietnam take Pnomh Penh and announce the collapse of the regime of dictator Pol Pot, who flees to the Thai border.

The Village People

January 1979

Monday 8: 50 people are killed when the French tanker Betelgeuse explodes at the Gulf Oil terminal in Bantry, County Cork, Ireland.

Tuesday 9: The Music for UNICEF fundraising concert is broadcast on TV around the world, featuring the Bee Gees, ABBA, Rod Stewart and Donna Summer.

Wednesday 10: Britain's *Sun* newspaper has the headline 'Crisis? What Crisis?' as Prime Minister James Callaghan denies the country is in difficulties following the industrial unrest of the 'Winter of Discontent'.

Thursday 11: The musical *The Grand Tour* by Jerry Herman opens on Broadway.

John McEnroe.

Friday 12: Over 100 people are killed as some of the worst blizzards on record hit the midwestern USA.

Saturday 13: The Young Mens' Christian Association (YMCA) announces it is suing the Village People for alleged misuse of its name in their hit song *YMCA*.

Sunday 14: John McEnroe beats Arthur Ashe in the ATP Masters Grand Prix tennis tournament at Madison Square Garden, New York City.

Monday 15: Tensions grow in Iran; only one third of the members of the Shah's newly installed parliament turn up for its first meeting.

Tuesday 16: Shah Mohammed Reza Pahlavi flees Iran with his family as the Iranian Revolution breaks out.

Wednesday 17: The first episode of the Noel Edmonds game show *Lucky Numbers* is broadcast on BBC TV.

Thursday 18: Travel writer Peter Jenkins completes his coast-to-coast walk across the USA, begun in October 1973.

The Shah of Iran.

Friday 19: Former US Attorney General John N Mitchell is released from prison after a 19 month sentence for his involvement in the Watergate affair.

Saturday 20: A million Iranians march in Tehran in support of exiled Islamic fundamentalist leader Ayatollah Khomeini.

Sunday 21: The planet Neptune begins a 20 year cycle as the outermost planet of the solar system, as Pluto's orbit moves closer to the sun.

The Ayatollah Khomeini.

January 1979

The General E Lee car featured in *The Dukes of Hazzard*.

Monday 22: In the biggest mass stoppage since the General Strike of 1926, public sector workers across the UK come out on strike for higher pay.

Tuesday 23: Negotiations between the British government and trade union leaders make little progress as unions call for an all-out national strike.

Wednesday 24: The US performs a nuclear test in Nevada.

Thursday 25: Pope John Paul II makes his first visit to Mexico for the 1979 Latin American Episcopal Conference.

Friday 26: Popular US TV series *The Dukes of Hazzard* is first shown on CBS.

Saturday 27: At the 36th Golden Globes Awards, John Voight wins Best Actor and Jane Fonda wins Best Actress, both for *Coming Home.*

Sunday 28: The musical *The Wiz*, based on L Frank Baum's *Wizard of Oz* books, closes at the Majestic Theatre in New York City after 1672 performances.

John Voight.

Monday 29: Brenda Ann Spencer kills two teachers and wounds eight pupils in a shooting at Cleveland Elementary School in San Diego, California. The incident inspires the Boomtown Rats song *I Don't Like Mondays.*

Tuesday 30: A Boeing 707 cargo aircraft, Varig Flight 967 goes missing with all six crew on route from Japan to Brazil; it is never found.

The Ayatollah arrives in Iran.

Wednesday 31: US guitarist Grant Green, known as 'the father of Acid Jazz', dies aged 43.

Thursday 1: The Ayatollah Khomeini returns to Iran after 15 years in exile.

Friday 2: Former Sex Pistols bassist Sid Vicious is found dead in New York of a heroin overdose following release from prison on bail.

Sid Vicious *(left)* is found dead.

Saturday 3: Ayatollah Khomeini creates the Councils of the Islamic Revolution.

Sunday 4: Italian Formula One racing driver Giorgio Pantano is born in Padua, Italy.

February 1979

Monday 5: Gulf and Western Industries publishes its 64 page annual report as an insert in *Time* magazine; costing $4m it is the most expensive print advertisement to this date.

Tuesday 6: Following a 1977 coup, the Supreme Court of Pakistan sentences former Prime Minister and President Zulfikar Ali Bhutto to death.

Wednesday 7: Nazi war criminal Josef Mengele, living in exile in Brazil, drowns while swimming; his remains are not found until 1985.

Trevor Francis: Britain's most expensive footballer.

Thursday 8: After a record 84 days in orbit, the crew of the space station Skylab 4 returns to Earth.

Rod Stewart.

Friday 9: British football's first £1m transfer takes place as Trevor Francis moves from Birmingham City to Nottingham Forest.

Saturday 10: *Do Ya Think I'm Sexy* by Rod Stewart reaches number one in the US charts; royalties are donated to UNICEF.

Sunday 11: The Iranian army hands over power to Ayatollah Khomeini, marking the end of the Pahlavi dynasty begun in 1925.

Former Beatle George Harrison.

Monday 12: The first episode of children's animated series *Bagpuss* airs on British TV.

Tuesday 13: Vigilante group The Guardian Angels is formed in New York City by Curtis Sliwa.

Wednesday 14: The US ambassador to Afghanistan, Adolph Dubs, is kidnapped by Islamic extremists in Kabul; Dubs is later killed in a shootout with police.

Thursday 15: In the 21st Grammy Awards, Billy Joel's *Just the Way You Are* is declared Song of the Year.

Friday 16: Ex-Beatle George Harrison releases the song *Blow Away*.

Saturday 17: The Sino-Vietnamese war breaks out as China invades Vietnam.

Sunday 18: For the first time in recorded history, snow falls in the Sahara Desert. Flakes fall for about 30 minutes in southern Algeria but rapidly melt away.

Cult British TV children's character Bagpuss, created by Peter Firmin and Oliver Postgate.

February 1979

Monday 19: HM Queen Elizabeth II undertakes a state visit to Saudi Arabia to meet with King Khalid.

Tuesday 20: 11 members of a Loyalist gang in Belfast known as the Shankhill Butchers, are sentenced to life for murder.

Wednesday 21: Japan launches the Hakucho X-Ray Astrononomy Satellite.

Thursday 22: St Lucia is granted independence from the United Kingdom.

General Frank Petersen Jr.

Friday 23: Frank Petersen Jr becomes the first black general in the United States Marine Corps.

Saturday 24: War begins between North and South Yemen.

Sunday 25: The USSR launches *Soyuz 32,* carrying two cosmonauts to the Salyut 6 space station.

A Soviet Soyuz spacecraft.

Total solar eclipse in Bozeman, Montana.

Monday 26: A solar eclipse takes place across the USA and Canada, with totality in the state of Montana. It is the last total eclipse before 2017.

Tuesday 27: Indian politician Sanjay Gandhi, son of Prime Minister Indira Gandhi, is sentenced to two year's imprisonment for destroying all copies of a film criticising him and his mother. The conviction is later overturned.

Wednesday 28: Ernest Thompson's play *On Golden Pond* opens on Broadway in New York City. It runs for 126 performances and is made into a film in 1981 starring Henry Fonda and Katherine Hepburn.

Thursday 1: Scotland votes in a referendum on devolution; the majority of votes are in favour but turnout is too low for the result to be valid. Wales votes against devolution.

Friday 2: A ceasefire for Saturday is announced in Yemen.

Saturday 3: It is announced Private First Class Robert Garwood, thought to be the last US prisoner of war held in Vietnam, will be released after 14 years in captivity.

Sunday 4: Up to 15 inches of torrential rain inundates the gulf coast and southeastern USA, causing widespread flooding and damage.

March 1979

Monday 5: NASA's *Voyager 1* probe makes its closest approach to Jupiter, photographing the planet's rings at 172,000 miles away.

Tuesday 6: Actor Charles Wagenheim (*Gunsmoke, All in the Family*) dies aged 83 after being attacked during a burglary.

Wednesday 7: In the 5th People's Choice Awards, Burt Reynolds wins Favorite Movie Actor and Olivia Newton John wins Favorite Movie Actress.

Burt Reynolds.

Thursday 8: Phillips demonstrates the prototype Compact Disc publicly for the first time.

Friday 9: France performs a nuclear test at Mururoa Atoll in the Pacific Ocean.

Saturday 10: *The Dukes of Hazzard* is first broadcast on BBC TV in the UK.

Sunday 11: Actor Victor Killian, aged 88, is killed by burglars just days after his fellow *All In the Family* cast member Charles Wagenheim dies in the same way.

The red spot of Jupiter as seen by *Voyager 1.*

Monday 12: The European Council meets in Paris and announces the implementation of the European Monetary System (EMS) which it says must be supported by 'increased convergence' of member states' economies.

Tuesday 13: The revolutionary marxist-leninist New Jewel Movement in the former British colony of Grenada overthrows the government of Prime Minister Eric Gairy.

Wednesday 14: At least 200 people are killed when a Hawker Siddeley Trident aeroplane crashes into a factory near Beijing (Peking), China.

Thursday 15: In cricket, Pakistan, captained by Majid Khan, beats Australia by 71 runs in the First Test at Melbourne, Australia.

Friday 16: CBS TV in the USA broadcasts *Wings over the World*, a documentary film about Paul McCartney's group Wings.

Paul and Linda McCartney of Wings.

Saturday 17: Two workers are killed when the Penmanshiel Tunnel collapses in Berwickshire, Scotland.

Sunday 18: Ten miners die in a methane gas explosion at Golborne Colliery near Wigan, England.

March 1979

Challenger is delivered.

Monday 19: Actor Richard Beckinsale (star of *Rising Damp* and *Porridge*, and father of actress Kate Beckinsale) dies aged 31 from a heart condition.

Tuesday 20: Maverick Italian journalist Mino Pecorelli, 50, is shot dead in Rome. The convictions of two Mafia members for his murder are later overturned and his killing remains unsolved.

Wednesday 21: The Egyptian Parliament approves a peace treaty with Israel; the Israeli Parliament reciprocates the next day.

Thursday 22: Sir Richard Sykes KCMG MC, British ambassador to the Netherlands, is assassinated by the IRA in The Hague; his manservant Karel Straub is also killed in the attack.

Friday 23: Paul McCartney's group Wings releases the single *Goodnight Tonight.*

Saturday 24: The new space shuttle *Columbia* is delivered to Kennedy Space Centre on the back of a jumbo jet.

Sunday 25: Martina Navratilova beats Tracey Austin in the WTA tennis championships in New York City.

Monday 26: Israeli Prime Minister Menachem Begin and Egyptian President Anwar Sadat sign the Eypt-Israel Peace Treaty in Washington, DC.

Anwar Sadat (left) with President Carter (centre) and Menachem Begin in Washington, DC.

Tuesday 27: The US Supreme Court rules in Delaware *v.* Prouse that it is unconstitutional for a police officer to stop a motorist without evidence or reasonable suspicion of a crime having been committed.

Wednesday 28: A coolant leakage takes place at the nuclear power plant at Three Mile Island in Pennsylvania, the worst accident in US nuclear history.

Thursday 29: Sultan Yahya Petra of Kelantan, ruler of Malaysia, dies in office. He is replaced by Sultan Ahmad Shah of Pahang.

Friday 30: British Member of Parliament and decorated war hero Lt Col Airey Neave DSO OBE MC is killed in an IRA car bomb attack in Westminster.

Saturday 31: Israel wins the Eurovision Song Contest with Gali Atari and Milk and Honey's song *Hallelujah*.

Sunday 1: The Shah of Iran is officially overthrown as Iran becomes an Islamic republic.

April 1979

Monday 2: 66 people are killed in Sverdlovsk, USSR, when a biowarfare laboratory accidentally releases anthrax spores.

London Transport's 1930s RT-type bus.

Tuesday 3: Jane M Byrne becomes the first woman mayor of Chicago, Illinois.

Wednesday 4: The former President of Pakistan, Zulfikar Ali Bhutto is executed.

Thursday 5: Talks collapse between management and unions at United Airlines, continuing a strike which lasts until May.

Archie Bunker, played by Carrol O'Connor.

Friday 6: Lord Frederick Windsor, son of Prince Michael of Kent and cousin of HM Queen Elizabeth II, is born in London.

Saturday 7: London Transport's last 'RT-type' buses (the forerunner of the classic 'Routemaster') are withdrawn from service.

Sunday 8: Long-running US sitcom *All In the Family*, featuring 'loveable bigot' Archie Bunker, ends after 204 episodes.

Monday 9: *The Deer Hunter* receives five Oscars at the 51st Academy Awards, which are presented by John Wayne in his final public appearance.

Tuesday 10: The Soviets launch the Soyuz 33 mission to their Salyut 6 space station; it later has to be aborted due to technical failure.

Wednesday 11: The Tanzanian army captures Kampala, forcing Ugandan dictator Idi Amin to flee into exile in Libya.

Idi Amin.

Thursday 12: Failed Soviet space mission Soyuz 33 returns to Earth.

Friday 13: The longest table tennis doubles match on record ends after 101 hours in Sacramento, California.

Saturday 14: Grenada and Cuba establish diplomatic relations.

Sunday 15: A major earthquake strikes parts of Yugoslavia and Albania, killing 136 people and devastating the town of Budva.

Collapsed hotel in Budva.

April 1979

Monday 16: Bill Rodgers of the USA wins the 83rd Boston Marathon in 2:09:27.

Tuesday 17: Four Royal Ulster Constabulary officers are killed by an IRA bomb in Bessbrooke, County Armagh.

Wednesday 18: Saad Haddad, commander of the Maronite Christian South Lebanon Army declares the setting up of the Free Lebanon State during the country's civil war.

James McAvoy, born on 21 April.

Thursday 19: Actress Kate Hudson (*Almost Famous, You, Me and Dupree*) is born in Los Angeles, California.

Friday 20: US President Jimmy Carter is attacked by a swamp rabbit while fishing at Plains, Georgia.

Saturday 21: Actor James McAvoy (*X-Men*) is born in Glasgow, Scotland.

Sunday 22: The Albert Einstein Memorial *(below)* is unveiled at the National Academy of Sciences in Washington, DC.

Monday 23: Anti-Nazi League demonstrator Blair Peach is fatally injured when fighting breaks out with the right-wing National Front in London, England. A later enquiry concludes Peach's injuries were 'almost certainly' caused by an unidentified police officer.

Tuesday 24: Bishop Abel Muzorewa becomes Prime Minister of Rhodesia.

Wednesday 25: John Graham, 55, serving with the Ulster Defence Regiment, is shot dead by an IRA sniper in Seskinore, County Tyrone.

Bishop Muzorewa.

Thursday 26: La Soufrière St Vincent volcano erupts in St Vincent in the West Indies, blanketing the island in ash but causing no casualties.

Friday 27: Former Beatle George Harrison releases *Love Comes to Everyone.*

Saturday 28: Polish composer Felix Labunski dies aged 86.

Sunday 29: *Reunited* by Peaches and Herb knocks Blondie's *Heart of Glass* off the US number one slot.

Musical duo Peaches and Herb.

April/May 1979

Monday 30: Mary Therese Friel of New York City is crowned Miss USA 1979.

Tuesday 1: Greenland is granted autonomy from Denmark.

Wednesday 2: Nobel Prize-winning Italian chemist Giulio Natta dies aged 76.

Thursday 3: Martin Sherman's play *Bent*, about the persecution of homosexuals in Nazi Germany, premieres in London.

Friday 4: Following the previous day's General Election in the United Kingdom, Margaret Thatcher of the Conservative Party becomes the country's first woman Prime Minister, replacing Labour's James Callaghan.

Saturday 5: The Voyager 1 space probe, launched in 1977, passes the planet Jupiter.

Sunday 6: Sergeant Robert Maughan, 30, of the 9/12 Lancers, and Detective Constable Norman Prue, 29, of the Royal Irish Constabulary are shot dead during an IRA ambush in Lisnaskea, County Fermanagh.

Margaret Thatcher.

James Callaghan.

Monday 7: Rhodesia's black majority parliament meets for the first time.

Tuesday 8: Ten people are killed when fire breaks out at a Woolworth's store in Manchester, England.

Wednesday 9: Civil war breaks out in El Salvador.

Thursday 10: The Federated States of Micronesia in the Pacific Ocean become self-governing.

The fire-damaged Woolworth's store in Manchester.

Friday 11: Eight men are missing presumed dead after an oil rig collapses in the Gulf of Mexico near Galveston, Texas.

Saturday 12: Tennis player Chris Evert ends her record-breaking run of 125 victories on clay courts when she loses to Tracy Austin in the Italian Open.

Sunday 13: Revolutionary leaders in Iran call for the death of the country's king, the Shah, exiled in January 1979.

Chris Evert.

May 1979

Monday 14: *The Kids Are Alright*, a 'rockumentary' about English band The Who, premieres at the Cannes Film Festival.

The Who in 1975.

Tuesday 15: HM Queen Elizabeth II opens Parliament: her new Conservative government pledges to cut income tax and reform the trade unions.

Wednesday 16: US President Carter expresses optimism that the country's fuel shortages will soon be over.

Thursday 17: Gasoline prices hit a record high of $1 per gallon in New York City.

Friday 18: Britain announces it will send an envoy to Rhodesia, in a tacit recognition of the new black-majority ruled state.

Saturday 19: Turkish and Greek Cypriot leaders agree to talks on Cyprus following Turkey's invasion of the island in 1974.

Sunday 20: Elton John arrives in Leningrad, becoming the first western pop star to play in the USSR.

Elton John.

Monday 21: Dan White is convicted of killing San Francisco Mayor George Moscone and Supervisor Harvey Milk in 1978.

Tuesday 22: The US Steel corporation agrees to spend $400m on reducing steelmaking pollution.

Wednesday 23: Hubert Van Doorne, founder of the Dutch motor company DAF and inventor of the 'Variomatic' transmission, dies aged 79.

Francis Ford Coppola.

Thursday 24: Francis Ford Coppola's Vietnam War film *Apocalypse Now* receives the Palme d'Or at the Cannes film festival.

Friday 25: 273 people are killed when an American Airlines DC-10 crashes on takeoff from O'Hare International Airport in Chicago. It remains the deadliest aviation accident in history.

Saturday 26: US actor George Brent (*Baby Face*) dies aged 75.

Sunday 27: Investigators announce that the DC-10 crash on 25 May was caused by metal fatigue on an engine bolt, and recommend that all DC-10s are grounded for checks.

DAF car with 'Variomatic' transmission.

Hubert Van Doorne.

May/June 1979

Monday 28: Greece gains accession to the European Economic Community (forerunner of the EU).

Tuesday 29: Silent screen legend Mary Pickford dies aged 87.

Wednesday 30: To highlight transport alternatives in the energy crisis, technology author Ted Coombs begins a 5,193 mile journey across the USA on roller skates.

Thursday 31: The first computer analysis of welfare recipients in New York State reveals widespread fraud, with around 25% of claims being made falsely.

Friday 1: Heavy fighting breaks out in Nicaragua as Sandanista rebels attempt to overthrow the rule of General Anastasio Somozo.

Pope John Paul II

Saturday 2: Pope John Paul II arrives in Poland, the first Pope in office to visit a communist country.

Sunday 3: One of the worst oil spills on record takes place in the Gulf of Mexico as the Ixtoc well explodes, causing widespread ecological damage.

The Ixtoc oil spill.

Monday 4: Joseph Clark becomes Canada's youngest Prime Minister, aged just 39.

Tuesday 5: US President Carter meets with representatives of NASA to agree funding for the 1981 Space Shuttle programme.

Wednesday 6: Actor Jack Haley (the Tin Man in *The Wizard of Oz*) dies aged 80.

Joseph Clark.

Thursday 7: The first international elections in history take place, as voters elect members of the European Parliament.

Friday 8: Robert Mugabe, leader of anti-government guerilla forces in Zimbabwe-Rhodesia, states that war in the country will be prolonged if the US and UK lift sanctions against the new government.

Jack Haley (right) at the 1970 *Wizard of Oz* reunion.

Saturday 9: Britain's Michael Cairney sets the world record for domino-toppling as he knocks over 169,713 in 40 minutes in a charity event at Poughkeepsie, NY.

Sunday 10: Tennis star Chris Evert defeats Wendy Turnbull to win her third singles crown in the French Open.

Robert Mugabe.

June 1979

Monday 11: Rock and roll singer Chuck Berry is sentenced to four months' imprisonment for tax evasion.

Tuesday 12: Bryan Allen rides the Gossamer Albatross pedal-powered aeroplane across the English Channel in 2h 14m.

Wednesday 13: US courts rule that the US government's seizure of the Black Hills of Dakota from the Sioux Indians in 1877 was illegal. $106m compensation is offered but refused by the tribe.

Thursday 14: Canada are all out for 45 runs in the Cricket World Cup against England.

Friday 15: *Rocky II* starring Sylvester Stallone is released.

Sylvester Stallone.

Saturday 16: Eight senior Nigerian army officers are executed by firing squad on charges of corruption.

Sunday 17: Sunni Islamist terrorists linked to the Muslim Brotherhood kill 32 army cadets in Aleppo, Syria.

The *Gossamer Albatross.*

Monday 18: US President Carter *(above, left)* and the USSR's Leonid Brezhnev sign the SALT II agreement limiting nuclear arms proliferation.

Tuesday 19: Marais Viljoen becomes President of South Africa.

Wednesday 20: ATV news correspondent Bill Stewart and his interpreter, Juan Espinosa, are killed by Nicaraguan soldiers while reporting on the communist uprising in the country. The incident inspires the 1983 film *Under Fire*, starring Gene Hackman.

Thursday 21: US President Carter orders the FBI to maintain order as a nationwide truck drivers' strike worsens.

Friday 22: *The Muppet Movie* is released in the USA.

Saturday 23: The West Indies beat England by 92 runs to win the Cricket World Cup.

Sunday 24: The fuel crisis continues in the USA, with over 95% of filling stations closed in the New York area.

June/July 1979

Monday 25: The Commander of NATO forces in Europe, General Alexander Haig, survives an assassination attempt in Belgium. A member of the Baader-Meinhof terrorist group is later found guilty of the attack.

Tuesday 26: The 11th James Bond film, *Moonraker*, starring Roger Moore, premieres in London.

Wednesday 27: Boxer Muhammed Ali announces his retirement.

Roger Moore.

Thursday 28: German composer Paul Dessau dies aged 84.

Sony Walkman.

Friday 29: Libya's leader Colonel Gadaffi announces that his country will halt oil exports for two years, adding to the west's energy crisis.

Saturday 30: The hit song *Good Times* by Chic is released on 45 rpm single in the USA.

Sunday 1: The iconic Sony Walkman compact personal cassette player is launched. The first lightweight portable stereo cassette player, it becomes a huge worldwide success.

Monday 2: The first US coin (one dollar) to depict a woman, the suffragette Susan B Anthony, is issued.

Tuesday 3: French composer Louis Durey, an early exponent of Schoenberg's 'twelve-tone' technique, dies aged 91.

Wednesday 4: Algeria's former President Ben Bella, deposed in 1965, is released from house arrest.

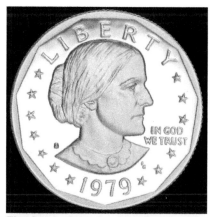

The Susan B Anthony dollar.

Thursday 5: Queen Elizabeth II attends the 1000th anniversary of the founding of the Isle of Man's parliament, the Tynewald.

Friday 6: An IRA bomb explodes in the British consulate in Antwerp, Belgium; no-one is injured.

Saturday 7: Björn Borg beats the USA's Roscoe Tanner to win his fourth consecutive Wimbledon tennis title.

Sunday 8: The *Voyager 2* space probe takes the first ever photograph of Jupiter's tiny moon, Adrastea.

Björn Borg.

July 1979

Monday 9: A bomb destroys the unoccupied car of Nazi hunters Serge and Beate Klarsfield at their home in France. A note claiming responsibility purporting to be from a group of former SS officers is found at the scene.

Tuesday 10: In response to the energy crisis, US President Carter announces that public buildings may not be air-conditioned to below 78F (25C) or heated to above 65F (18C).

The Skylab space station.

Wednesday 11: Amid huge media attention, NASA's decommissioned Skylab space station, in decaying orbit, breaks up in the Earth's atmosphere. Most pieces of the wreckage fall harmlessly nto the Indian Ocean but some are also found in parts of the Australian outback.

Thursday 12: Kiribati (formerly the Gilbert Islands) is granted independence from the United Kingdom.

Friday 13: The International Whaling Commission in London votes against a worldwide whaling ban but votes in favour of establishing a whale sanctuary in the Indian Ocean.

Saturday 14: Germany's world champion figure skater Robin Szolkowy is born in Greifswald, East Germany.

Sunday 15: US President Carter addresses the nation in a televised speech about the lack of confidence in the country. It becomes known as his 'national malaise' speech.

Monday 16: Iraq's President Hasan al-Bakr resigns and is replaced by Vice President Saddam Hussein.

Tuesday 17: Nicaragua's dictator General Anastasio Somozo Debayle flees to Miami.

Donna Summer.

Wednesday 18: The USSR performs a nuclear test at Semipalitinsk in Eastern Kazakh.

Thursday 19: Several people are injured when the stage collapses following the crowning of Maritza Sayalero, 18, of Venezuela, as 'Miss Universe' in Perth, Australia.

Vietnamese boat people.

Friday 20: The United Nations holds talks in Geneva to discuss the increasing problem of refugees known as the 'boat people' attempting to leave war-torn Vietnam by sea.

Saturday 21: The disco craze reaches its peak, with disco songs in the top six places of the US charts. Donna Summer's *Bad Girls* is at number one.

Sunday 22: Saddam Hussein purges nearly seventy members of his ruling Ba'ath party; most are later executed.

July 1979

Monday 23:
Following a dispute with the government over flooding, a group of farmers in Victoria, Australia, declare their land the Independent State of Rainbow Creek, an autonomous British colony with HM Queen Elizabeth II as head of state. The status of the area remains unresolved to this day.

Ted Bundy in court.

Tuesday 24: Notorious US serial killer Ted Bundy is convicted by a Florida jury. He confesses to 30 murders of young women carried out between 1974 and 1978, keeping the severed heads of some victims in his apartment. He is sentenced to death and eventually executed by electric chair in 1989.

Wednesday 25: Israel returns a 2,500 square mile area of the Sinai Desert to Egypt as part of a staged withdrawal from territories seized in the Arab-Israeli war.

Thursday 26: Britain's new Conservative government announces plans to privatise the British National Oil Corporation (BNOC).

Friday 27: Following a slump in sales, General Motors in the USA lays off 12,600 workers and announces a cutback in the production of 1980 models.

Saturday 28: Charan Singh is installed as India's fifth Prime Minister, heading a three-party coalition government.

Sunday 29: Four people are killed and 113 injured in Basque separatists bomb attacks in Madrid, Spain.

Monday 30: The discovery of the largest dinosaur on record is announced by Dr James Jensen of Brigham Young University, Utah; the Brachiosaurus, found in Colorado, is thought to have been about 60 feet tall and weighed 80 tons.

Tuesday 31: The Carter administration unveils plans for its Charter for the Federal Bureau of Information (FBI) which will govern the Bureau and restrict controversial practices such as covert activity and use of informants.

Wednesday 1: As the fuel crisis continues, General Motors announces its 1985 models will be its most economical yet, with at least 27.5 mpg in fuel consumption.

Thursday 2: Disgraced former US President Richard Nixon cancels plans to buy an apartment in Manhattan after objections from neighbours.

Former US President Richard Nixon.

Friday 3: At a meeting of Commonwealth leaders in Zambia, Britain's Prime Minister Margaret Thatcher indicates that the UK may not lift sanction against Zimbabwe-Rhodesia unless it alters its constitution.

Saturday 4: The first ever league game of American Football is played in West Germany, between Frankfurter Löwen and Düsseldorf Panther.

Sunday 5: Heavy fighting breaks out in Afghanistan between rebel army units and troops loyal to communist leader President Noor Muhammed Taraki.

August 1979

Monday 6: Schoolboy Marcus Hooper becomes the youngest person to swim the English Channel, aged just 12.

Tuesday 7: United Nations and Red Cross representatives report that 2.25 million Cambodians face starvation following the country's war with Vietnam.

Wednesday 8: US commercial divers Richard Walker and Victor Guiel die of hypothermia after their diving bell becomes stranded at a depth of over 160 metres (520 ft) in the East Shetland Basin. The accident leads to important safety changes in the diving industry.

Thursday 9: American gangster Raymond Lee Washington, founder of the notorious Crips gang, is killed in a drive-by shooting in Los Angeles.

Friday 10: Michael Jackson releases his breakthrough album, *Off the Wall.* It goes on to sell over seven million copies and becomes Billboard Album of the Year.

Saturday 11: The Carter administration steps up efforts to prevent Pakistan from developing nuclear weapons.

Sunday 12: China announces its stringently enforced 'one child policy' to control population growth.

A Soviet ship brings food aid to famine-stricken Cambodia.

Monday 13: Five workmen are killed and 15 injured when the roof of the Rosemont Horizon (Allstate Arena) stadium collapses near Chicago, Illinois.

Tuesday 14: The largest British rescue operation in peacetime takes place when a freak storm hits the Fastnet yacht race, killing 19 people and shipwrecking 125 yachtsmen. Over 4000 personnel are involved in the rescue, including the Royal Navy and the Irish and Dutch navies.

Irish memorial to the 19 people killed in the Fastnet race.

Wednesday 15: The Vietnam war film *Apocalypse Now*, starring Marlon Brando and Martin Sheen, is released in the USA.

Thursday 16: John Diefenbaker, 13th Prime Minister of Canada, dies aged 83.

Marlon Brando.

Friday 17: The controversial religious comedy film *Monty Python's Life of Brian* premieres in the USA.

Saturday 18: Iranian troops crush a Kurdish revolt, acting on direct orders from the Ayatollah Khomeini, who goes over the heads of military leaders.

Sunday 19: Soviet Cosmonauts Vladimir Lyakov and Valery Ryumin return to Earth aboard Soyuz 34 after a record 175 days in orbit.

August 1979

Monday 20: The east coast main railway line from England to Scotland re-opens following the collapse of the Penmanshiel Tunnel in March.

Tuesday 21: Soviet dancer Alexander Godunov claims asylum in New York City while on tour with the Bolshoi Ballet. He later finds fame playing a German terrorist in the 1988 film *Die Hard.*

Stan Kenton

Wednesday 22: American novelist James T Farrell, author of the *Studs Lonigan* books about working class life in the 1930s, dies aged 75.

Thursday 23: Cricketer Mian Mohammed Saeed, Pakistan's first captain (1948-49) dies aged 68.

James T Farrell.

Friday 24: The 36th Venice Film Festival opens.

Saturday 25: Jazz musician and big band leader Stan Kenton dies aged 67.

Sunday 26: The UN announces a ceasefire in Lebanon between Lebanese Christian forces and the Palestinian Liberation Organisation will go into effect on Monday.

Monday 27: Former Viceroy of India Lord Louis Mountbatten is killed when an IRA bomb explodes on his boat at Mullaghmore, County Sligo. On the same day 18 British soldiers are killed in an IRA ambush at Warrenpoint, County Down.

Tuesday 28: Seven people are injured when an IRA bomb explodes in the main square of Brussels, Belgium, just before a British Army band concert is due to take place.

Earl Mountbatten of Burma.

Wednesday 29: British Prime Minister Margaret Thatcher makes a surprise visit to survivors of recent IRA violence in Belfast.

Thursday 30: Comet Howard-Koomen-Michels collides with the sun, causing a huge explosion; it is the only known comet to have made contact with the sun's surface.

Friday 31: 11 bank robberies take place in New York City, bringing the month's total to 137.

Saturday 1: The US space probe *Pioneer 11* becomes the first craft to approach Saturn, and discovers the moon Epimethius.

Sunday 2: The Transglobe Expedition begins. It is the first longitudinal (pole to pole) circum-navigation of the globe, led by explorers Ranulph Fiennes and Charles R Burton.

Artist's impression of *Pioneer 11*.

September 1979

Monday 3: Hurricane David hits Florida after causing at least 2000 deaths in the Caribbean. 400,000 Americans are evacuated in anticipation of the storm, although damage is less than expected.

Carly Simon, one of the stars at the MUSE concert.

Tuesday 4: In cricket, the Fourth Test ends in a draw between England and India at the Oval.

Wednesday 5: The ceremonial funeral of Lord Mountbatten, assassinated by the IRA on 27 August, is held in London's Westminster Abbey with the Queen and Royal Family in attendance.

Thursday 6: Ronald Binge, composer of BBC Radio Four's theme tune *Sailing By*, dies aged 69.

Friday 7: The four day MUSE (Musicians United for Safe Energy) anti-nuclear concert begins at Madison Square Garden in New York. Performers include Bruce Springsteen, Carly Simon and Chaka Khan.

Saturday 8: Cheryl Prewitt (22) is crowned the 52nd Miss America. She goes on to become a prolific writer on evangelical Christian topics.

Sunday 9: Tennis player John McEnroe beats Vitas Guerulaitas to win the first Grand Slam title in the US Men's Open.

Miss America, Cheryl Prewitt.

Monday 10: Teachers go on strike in 12 American states, with almost all 300 schools shut in Detroit, Michigan.

Tuesday 11: Britain's Conservative government announces plans to split the Post Office into two parts, the Royal Mail for post and British Telecom for telecommunications.

Wednesday 12: The tropical cyclone Hurricane Frederick hits the coast of Alabama, causing an estimated $1.7bn of damage across the eastern USA.

Thursday 13: South Africa declares the tiny state of Venda to be independent. Known as a 'Bantustan', such enclaves are condemned by the international community as being used as apartheid settlements for blacks.

The state of Venda *(top right)*.

Friday 14: Ted Coombs completes his 5,193 mile journey across the USA on roller skates, which he began on 30 May.

Saturday 15: US President Carter (55) drops out of a 10k (6.2 mile) running race in Catoctin, Maryland after collapsing from heat exhaustion.

Sunday 16: East Germans Peter Strelzyk and Gunter Wetzel and their families defect to the west in a home made hot-air balloon; the incident was later made into a film, *Night Crossing* starring John Hurt and Beau Bridges.

Beau Bridges.

September 1979

Monday 17: Italy's Pietro Mennea sets the world record for a 200 metres sprint (19.72s); it remains unbroken for 17 years.

Tuesday 18: The US Environmental Protection Agency announces that only two American cars (the Dodge Colt and Plymouth Champ) are in the world's top ten for fuel economy.

Wednesday 19: Firefighters battle with brush fires across 90,000 acres of countryside in California.

Thursday 20: David Dacko, former President of the Central African Republic, is restored to power following a coup against the self-proclaimed Emperor Bokassa, who seized power in 1966.

Friday 21: NASA launches its High Energy Astronomy Observatory (HEAO) 3 into orbit, to monitor cosmic rays.

Saturday 22: Two RAF Harrier jets collide while flying over Cambridgeshire, England; the pilots eject safely but three people are killed when the planes hit the ground near Wisbech.

Sunday 23: The Vela Incident or the South Atlantic Flash takes place: satellites observe two large unidentified flashes of light occuring in Antarctica. It is suspected to be a secret nuclear weapons test by South Africa and Israel.

Artist's impression of HEAO 3.

Monday 24: Soviet figure skater Oleg Protopopov and his wife Ludmila Belousova defect while on tour in Switzerland.

Tuesday 25: The Andrew Lloyd Webber musical *Evita!* transfers from London to Broadway, where it runs for 1568 performances.

Wednesday 26: A US government sponsored study shows that 40% of men who served in the Vietnam War now suffer from 'major emotional difficulties'.

Thursday 27: Veteran British singer and actress Dame Gracie Fields dies aged 81.

Gracie Fields.

Friday 28: Larry Holmes beats Earnie Shavers to gain the World Heavyweight boxing title.

Saturday 29: Pope John Paul II becomes the first pope to visit Ireland; he celebrates mass in an outdoor service in Dublin attended by 1.25m people.

Sunday 30: At midnight the US overseas territory surrounding the Panama Canal is handed over to Panamanian control. The canal itself remains under US control until 1999.

The cross in Croke Park, Dublin which marks the spot where Pope John Paul II held mass.

October 1929

Monday 1: Pope John Paul II arrives in Boston during his state visit to the USA.

The Pope in New York.

Tuesday 2: Over 80,000 attend a mass celebrated by Pope John Paul II at the Yankees Stadium in New York City.

Wednesday 3: A draft constitution is proposed for Zimbabwe-Rhodesia at the governmental conference on the colony's future in London.

Thursday 4: Soviet premier Leonid Brezhnev arrives in East Germany as part of celebrations for the country's 30th anniversary as a Communist state.

Friday 5: After a period of minor celebrity as 'America's oldest man', Mr Charlie Smith of Bartow, Florida, dies at the reputed age of 137. Later research shows that he was in fact only 100.

Saturday 6: Pope John Paul II becomes the first pope to visit the White House in Washington DC.

Sunday 7: National Guard troops are required to quell violent protestors at a nuclear plant in Seabrook, New Hampshire.

Monday 8: Singer Kenny Rogers wins Male Vocalist of the Year in the Country Music Association Awards.

Tuesday 9: Radio DJ Howard Stern, pioneer of the 'shock jock' style of presenting, begins his broadcasting career on WCCC in Hartford, Connecticut.

Wednesday 10: The US government announces that fuel stockpiles are sufficient for the coming winter, which makes an early appearance with snowfall in New York City.

Thursday 11: Large areas of downtown New York City are closed to traffic as Cuban leader Fidel Castro attends a meeting at the United Nations, his first visit to the USA in 19 years.

Friday 12: Typhoon Tip reaches 870 millibars off the coast of Guam in the Pacific Ocean; making it the most powerful tropical cyclone in history; 99 people are killed during widespread flooding caused by the storm.

Saturday 13: Cuban leader Fidel Castro calls for closer relations with the USA and the re-establishment of diplomatic links.

Sunday 14: 100,000 people protest in Bonn, capital of West Germany, *(below),* against the use of nuclear energy.

October 1979

Monday 15: President Carlos Romero is ousted from power and forced to flee the country during a coup in El Salvador.

Tuesday 16: The comedy sketch show *Not the Nine O'Clock News*, starring Rowan Atkinson and Mel Smith, makes its debut on BBC TV.

Wednesday 17: Mother Theresa of Calcutta is awarded the Nobel Peace Prize.

Mother Theresa.

Thursday 18: The London conference on the future of Zimbabwe-Rhodesia confirms that white farmers will not be compensated if their lands are appropriated by a new government.

Friday 19: 13 US Marines die in a fire caused by Typhoon Tip at Camp Fuji, Japan.

Mel Smith.

Saturday 20: John Tate of the USA defeats South Africa's Gerrie Coetzee to gain the MBA Heavyweight boxing title.

Sunday 21: Israel's Minister of Foreign Affairs, Moshe Dayan, resigns over the treatment of Palestinian territories within Israel; he goes on to form a new party, Telem, in 1981.

Moshe Dayan.

Monday 22: Capital punishment resumes in the state of Nevada after 18 years when multiple murderer Jesse Walter Bishop is executed.

Tuesday 23: The exiled Shah of Iran is treated for a blocked bile duct in a New York City hospital after being admitted in secret on Monday.

Wednesday 24: The Guinness Book of Records presents Paul McCartney with a Rhodium Disc, naming him as the best selling singer-songwriter of all time.

Thursday 25: A record price is fetched for an American painting when *The Icebergs* (1861) by Frederick Edwin Church is sold at auction for $2.5m.

The Icebergs.

Friday 26: South Korea's President, Park Chung Hee, is assassinated by the head of the country's security services, Kim Jae-gyu.

Saturday 27: The Caribbean islands of St Vincent and the Grenadines are granted independence from the United Kingdom.

Sunday 28: Warrant Officer David Bellamy, 31, of the Duke of Wellington's Regiment is killed in an IRA ambush in Belfast.

October/November 1979

Monday 29: Police arrest around 1,000 anti-nuclear demonstrators attempting to shut down the New York Stock Exchange.

Tuesday 30: British scientist Sir Barnes Wallis, inventor of the Bouncing Bomb (featured in the film *The Dambusters*), dies aged 92.

Wednesday 31: 71 people are killed when a DC-10 Western Airlines jet crash lands at Mexico City airport.

Thursday 1: Bolivia's General Alberto Natusch seizes control of the government in a military coup.

Friday 2: Peter Schaffer's play *Amadeus*, about the life of Mozart, opens at the National Theatre in London.

Saturday 3: Five members of the Communist Workers' Party are killed during a shoot-out with Ku Klux Klan members in Greensboro, North Carolina.

Sunday 4: The Iran Hostage Crisis begins as 500 Iranian Islamic radicals seize the US Embassy in Tehran and take 53 Americans hostage, demanding the Shah of Iran be returned to stand trial. The siege lasts for 444 days.

Iranian students attack the US Embassy in Tehran during the hostage crisis.

Ted Kennedy (left) with President Carter.

Monday 5: The Ayatollah Khomeini assumes dictatorial power in Iran and declares the USA to be 'the Great Satan'.

Tuesday 6: Oil prices soar when it is reported that Iran has stopped the loading of all tankers at its ports.

Wednesday 7: US Senator Ted Kennedy, brother of John F Kennedy, announces he will stand against Jimmy Carter in the 1980 Presidential Election.

Thursday 8: It is announced in London that some sanctions against Zimbabwe-Rhodesia will be dropped.

Friday 9: Four men are convicted of the murder of 13 year old Carl Bridgewater, shot dead after witnessing a robbery on his paper round in Stourbridge, England, in September 1978.

Saturday 10: The largest peacetime evacuation in Canadian history takes place when a train carrying explosives and dangerous chemicals explodes near Mississuaga, Ontario.

Sunday 11: British Prime Minister Margaret Thatcher announces major changes to the government of Northern Ireland, including the return of limited home rule.

November 1979

Monday 12: US President Carter announces a halt to all Iranian oil imports and a freeze on all Iranian assets.

Tuesday 13: *The Times* newspaper is published in London again after ceasing publication for almost a year during a strike.

Wednesday 14: The United Nations demands that Vietnamese forces withdraw from Cambodia.

Thursday 15: Britain's Prime Minister Margaret Thatcher reveals that the Surveyor of the Queen's Pictures, Sir Anthony Blunt, was a Soviet spy during the Second World War.

Friday 16: Paul McCartney and Wings release their hit single *Wonderful Christmas Time.*

Saturday 17: 13 hostages, all women or black men, are released from the US embassy in Tehran, Iran, as the Ayatollah Khomeini describes them as 'oppressed minorities'.

Sunday 18: Ronald Reagan's decision to stand against Jimmy Carter in the 1980 Presidential elections is supported in a straw poll at the Florida Republican Convention.

Anti-Iranian demonstration in New York during the hostage crisis.

Monday 19: Rock and roll singer Chuck Berry is released from prison following his incarceration for tax evasion.

Tuesday 20: 200 militants seize the Grand Mosque in Mecca, the holiest site in Islam, in protest against the Saudi monarchy.

Wednesday 21: The Ayatollah Khomeini claims on the radio that Americans have taken over the Grand Mosque, leading to a mob attack on the US embassy in Pakistan in which four people are killed.

Chuck Berry.

Thursday 22: England's soccer team defeats Bulgaria 2-0 in the qualifying round of the European Cup at Wembley Stadium, London.

Friday 23: In Dublin, IRA member Thomas McMahon is sentenced to life imprisonment for the murder of Lord Mountbatten in August.

Saturday 24: 250 people are killed as French special forces eject the Islamic militants from the Grand Mosque in Mecca.

Sunday 25: US sports commentators Pat Summerall and John Madden begin their 22 year broadcasting partnership.

Saudi troops storm the Grand Mosque.

November/December 1979

Monday 26: The Olympic Commission votes to readmit China to the Olympic Games after a 21-year ban.

Tuesday 27: The first one-day international cricket match played at night and with coloured strips takes place in Melbourne as Australia play the West Indies.

Wednesday 28: 257 people are killed when an Air New Zealand DC-10 airliner crashes into Mount Erebus on Antarctica. It remains New Zealand's deadliest peacetime disaster.

Thursday 29: Rock opera album *The Wall* by Pink Floyd is released.

Joyce Grenfell.

Friday 30: British comedienne Joyce Grenfell OBE dies aged 69.

Saturday 1: Following the death of three people in a car fire in Elkhart, Indiana, the state of Indiana announces it is suing the Ford motor company, claiming it failed to take corrective action over unsafe fuel tanks in its Pinto model.

Sunday 2: Demonstrators storm the US Embassy in Libya; the embassy staff escape unharmed.

The Ford Pinto.

Monday 3: Eleven people are killed during a rush for unreserved seating at a concert by The Who in Cincinnati, Ohio.

Tuesday 4: Three people are killed during a house fire in Hull, England. Police establish it was started deliberately by Bruce George Peter Lee, 19, who confesses to other arson attacks in which 26 people died, making him Britain's most prolific killer to that date.

Charles Haughey.

Wednesday 5: Jack Lynch resigns as *Taoiseach* (Prime Minister) of the Republic of Ireland; he is replaced by Charles Haughey.

Thursday 6: The world premiere of *Star Trek: the Motion Picture* starring William Shatner and Leonard Nimoy, is held at the Smithsonian Institution in Washington, DC.

Friday 7: Prince Shariar Shafiq, nephew of the deposed Shah of Iran and exiled leader of the Iranian resistance to Islamic takeover, is assassinated outside his home in Paris, France.

Leonard Nimoy as Mr Spock in *Star Trek*.

Saturday 8: The worldwide eradication of the smallpox virus is confirmed, making it one of only two diseases (the other being Rinderpest) to be completely eliminated.

Sunday 9: Prominent Roman Catholic Archbishop Fulton J Sheen, presenter of NBC's *Life is Worth Living*, dies aged 84.

December 1979

Monday 10: Mass arrests of pro-democracy campaigners take place in Taiwan after the country's first Human Rights Day is celebrated.

Tuesday 11: Six people are injured when a Cuban anti-Castro group explodes a bomb at the Soviet Mission to the United Nations in Manhattan.

Wednesday 12: The unrecognised state of Zimbabwe-Rhodesia returns to British control and is renamed Southern Rhodesia.

Thursday 13: US President Jimmy Carter meets with the newly formed Price Advisory Committee to discuss national wage levels.

Friday 14: The Chrysler motor company announces it will be bankrupt within a month, unless it is able to work out a rescue package with the US government.

Saturday 15: Canadian journalists Chris Haney and Scott Abbott create the prototype of the board game Trivial Pursuit.

Sunday 16: The USA beats Italy 5-0 in the final of the Davis Cup tennis tournament in Rome.

Trivial Pursuit.

The Klein Matterhorn cable car.

Monday 17: The Budweiser Rocket Car sets the world land speed record at 731.9 mph (1,117.9 kph) at Edwards Air Force Base, California; the claim is later disputed by experts.

Tuesday 18: New Romantic band Joy Division record their live album *Les Bains Douches.*

Wednesday 19: *Kramer* v *Kramer* starring Dustin Hoffmann and Meryl Streep is released (It is later voted Best Picture of 1980).

Thursday 20: The Jewish Theological Seminary of America votes 25-19 against the ordination of women as rabbis.

Friday 21: The Lancaster House Agreement in London declares a ceasefire between black nationalists and government forces in Southern Rhodesia.

Saturday 22: Hollywood movie mogul Darryl F Zanuck of 20th Century Fox dies aged 77.

Sunday 23: The Klein Matterhorn cable car opens, the highest in the world at 12,530 ft (3820m).

Monday 24: The first Ariane European Space Agency rocket is launched.

Tuesday 25: Hollywood actress Joan Blondell dies aged 73.

Wednesday 26: Following their invasion of Afghanistan, Soviet special forces take over the Presidential Palace in Kabul, killing the President, Hafizullah Amin, the following day.

Thursday 27: The soap opera *Knots Landing*, a spin-off of *Dallas*, first airs on CBS-TV. It goes on to become the third longest-running primetime drama on US TV.

Ariane 1.

Friday 28: US President Carter announces that the Soviet intervention in Afghanistan is a 'grave threat to peace'.

Saturday 29: In a telephone conversation with Soviet premier Leonid Brezhnev, US President Carter hints that he may provide funding for Islamic rebel forces.

Sunday 30: Composer Richard Rogers of musical duo Rogers and Hammerstein dies aged 77.

James Houghton and Kim Lankford as Kenny and Ginger Ward in *Knots Landing*.

Monday 31: A national British steelworkers' strike, the first in fifty years, is announced for Wednesday 2 January.

Birthday Notebooks
...a great alternative to a card.

Handy 60 page ruled notebooks with a significant event from the year heading each page.

Available from Montpelier Publishing at Amazon.

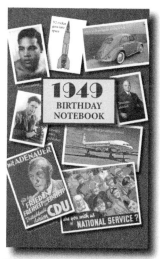

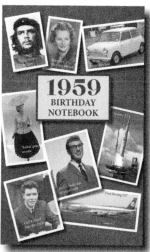

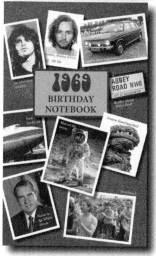

Printed in Great
Britain
by Amazon